KS2
9–10
Years

Master Maths at Home

Graphs and Measuring

Scan the QR code to help your child's learning at home.

 | **MATHS**
NO PROBLEM!

How to use this book

Maths — No Problem! created **Master Maths at Home** to help children develop fluency in the subject and a rich understanding of core concepts.

Key features of the Master Maths at Home books include:

- Carefully designed lessons that provide structure, but also allow flexibility in how they're used.

- Speech bubbles containing content designed to spark diverse conversations, with many discussion points that don't have obvious 'right' or 'wrong' answers.

- Rich illustrations that will guide children to a discussion of shapes and units of measurement, allowing them to make connections to the wider world around them.

- Exercises that allow a flexible approach and can be adapted to suit any child's cognitive or functional ability.

- Clearly laid-out pages that encourage children to practise a range of higher-order skills.

- A community of friendly and relatable characters who introduce each lesson and come along as your child progresses through the series.

You can see more guidance on how to use these books at **mastermathsathome.com**.

We're excited to share all the ways you can learn maths!

Copyright © 2022 Maths — No Problem!

Maths — No Problem!
mastermathsathome.com
www.mathsnoproblem.com
hello@mathsnoproblem.com

First published in Great Britain in 2022 by
Dorling Kindersley Limited
One Embassy Gardens, 8 Viaduct Gardens, London SW11 7BW
A Penguin Random House Company

The authorised representative in the EEA is Dorling Kindersley
Verlag GmbH. Arnulfstr. 124, 80636 Munich, Germany

10 9 8 7 6 5 4 3 2 1
001–327103–May/22

This book was made with Forest Stewardship Council™ certified paper - one small step in DK's commitment to a sustainable future. For more information go to www.dk.com/our-green-pledge

A CIP catalogue record for this book is available from the British Library.

ISBN: 978-0-24153-948-4
Printed and bound in the UK

For the curious
www.dk.com

Acknowledgements
The publisher would like to thank the authors and consultants Andy Psarianos, Judy Hornigold, Adam Gifford and Dr Anne Hermanson.

The Castledown typeface has been used with permission from the Colophon Foundry.

Contents

Ruby   Elliott   Amira   Charles   Lulu   Sam   Oak   Holly   Ravi   Emma   Jacob   Hannah

Understanding tables

Starter

Miss A'liya and Miss Fathima look at the gym timetable to plan which classes to go to.

Class	Start times	Duration (min)	Location
Superspin	09:35, 11:15, 13:05, 17:50	35	Room 2 (Level 3)
Skiparama	06:05, 08:25, 10:10, 20:45	30	Room 3 (Level 1)
Stretchathon	07:35, 11:15, 16:55, 21:25	45	Room 5 (Level 2)
Up and down	13:50, 19:10, 22:05	40	Room 1 (Level 3)
Twist 'n' turn	08:10, 09:10, 13:15	60	Room 4 (Level 1)

*Please arrive at the exercise class 5 minutes before the start time.
**Allow 2 minutes to travel between each floor.

If Miss A'liya and Miss Fathima want to go to 2 classes each, which classes should they choose?

Example

Miss A'liya wants to go to Superspin and Skiparama in the morning.

If I go to the 09:35 Superspin class, can I go to the 10:10 Skiparama class?

Miss A'liya needs to allow 4 minutes to travel between 2 floors.

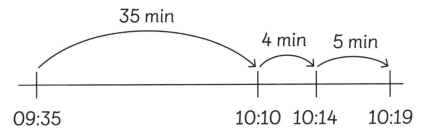

09:35   10:10 10:14   10:19

Miss A'liya needs to be at the 10:10 Skiparama class 5 minutes before it starts at 10:05. She cannot attend both the 09:35 Superspin and 10:10 Skiparama class.

Miss Fathima plans to go to the 11:15 Stretchathon class and stay at the gym for lunch. She will then go to the 13:50 Up and down class.
How much time will Miss Fathima spend at the gym?

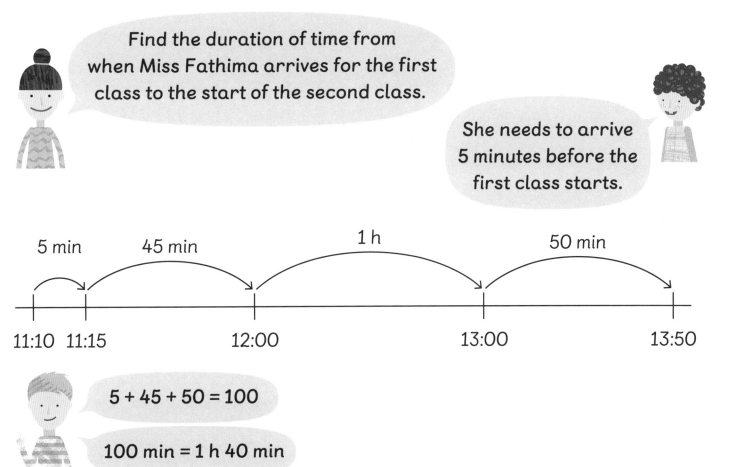

Find the duration of time from when Miss Fathima arrives for the first class to the start of the second class.

She needs to arrive 5 minutes before the first class starts.

5 + 45 + 50 = 100

100 min = 1 h 40 min

1 h 40 min + 1 h = 2 h 40 min

The duration of time from when Miss Fathima arrives for the first class to the start of the second class is 2 hours 40 minutes.

Add the duration of the Up and down class.

2 h 40 min + 40 min = 2 h 80 min
$\qquad\qquad\qquad$ = 3 h 20 min

80 min = 1 h 20 min

Miss Fathima will be at the gym for 3 hours 20 minutes.

Practice

Use the table in the Starter section to answer the following questions.

1 Sam's mum starts an Up and down class at 19:10.
How long does she have to sit down and rest before she has to leave for the 20:45 Skiparama class?

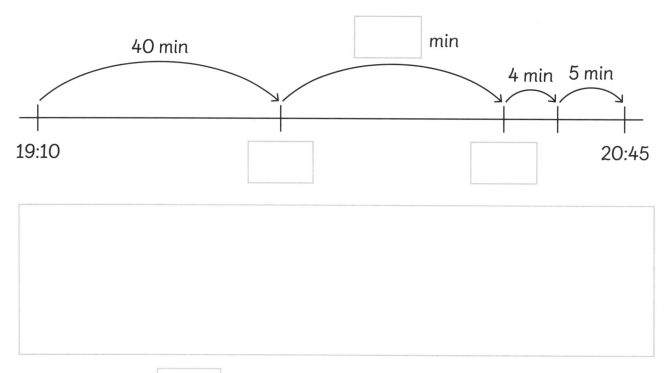

Sam's mum has ⬚ minutes to sit down and rest.

2 Mr Nightingale leaves the gym after he attends the 11:15 Stretchathon class. If he goes to a Superspin class before he goes to the Stretchathon class, for how long is he at the gym?

Mr Nightingale is at the gym for ⬚ hours ⬚ minutes.

3 Amira's dad arrives 15 minutes before his Up and down class starts. He talks to his friend for 55 minutes after the class finishes and then leaves the gym.
How much time has Amira's dad spent at the gym?

Amira's dad has spent ⬚ hours ⬚ minutes at the gym.

Line graphs (part 1)

Starter

The graph below shows the average monthly temperatures between 1980–2010 in Alexandra, New Zealand.

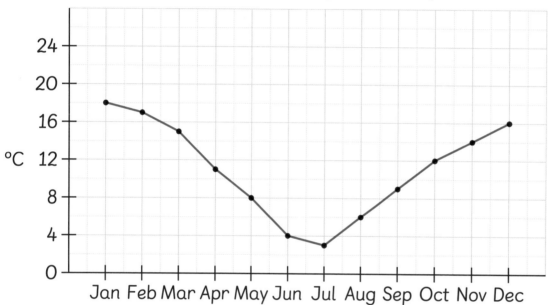

What can we say about the average monthly temperatures during this period?

Example

A line graph can show us changes over time.

The line graph shows the average monthly temperatures gradually decreased from January to July and then increased from July to December.
As the seasons change, so does the average monthly temperature.

We can also show the information on the graph in a table.

Month	Jan	Feb	Mar	Apr	May	Jun	Jul	Aug	Sep	Oct	Nov	Dec
°C	18	17	15	11	8	4	3	6	9	12	14	16

The highest average monthly temperature was in January.

The lowest average monthly temperature was in July.

Between January and June, the average monthly temperature decreased by 14 °C.

Between June and December, the average monthly temperature increased by 12 °C.

The greatest increase in the average temperature from one month to the next was 3 °C.

The greatest decrease in the average temperature from one month to the next was 4 °C.

1   The line graph below shows the average monthly temperatures in Christchurch, New Zealand, between 1980–2010.

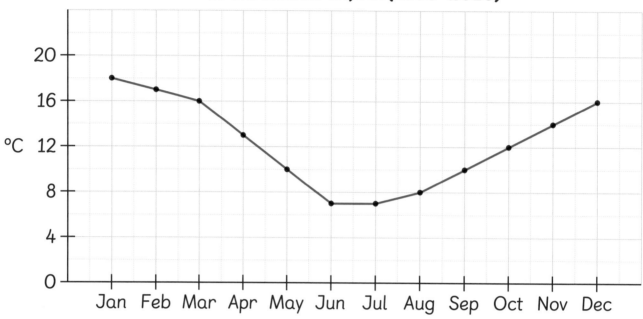

(a) The month with the highest average monthly temperature was

.

(b) The months with the lowest average monthly temperature were

and   .

(c) The difference between the highest and lowest average monthly

temperatures was   °C.

(d) The average monthly temperature decreased by   °C

between January and June.

2 Charles took the temperature at different times during one day in spring.

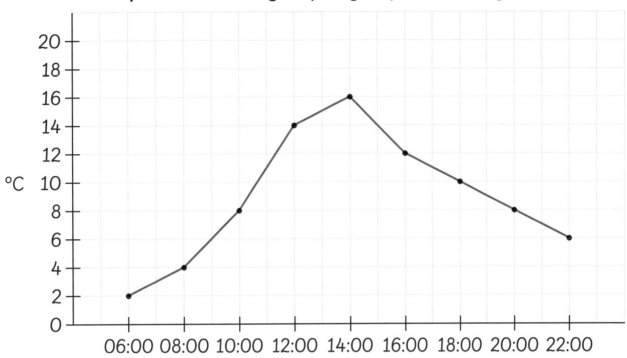

Temperature During a Spring Day in Tunbridge Wells, UK

(a) The difference in temperatures at 06:00 and 22:00 was [ ] °C.

(b) The temperature [ ] (increased / decreased) between 06:00 and 14:00.

(c) The temperature [ ] (increased / decreased) between 14:00 and 22:00.

(d) Between 10:00 and 12:00, the temperature increased by [ ] °C.

(e) Between 16:00 and 22:00, the temperature decreased at a rate of [ ] °C every 2 hours.

(f) The temperature increased by 14 °C between [ ] and [ ] .

Line graphs (part 2)

Starter

The graph below shows the average monthly temperatures between 1980–2010 in Alexandra, New Zealand and Rochdale, United Kingdom.

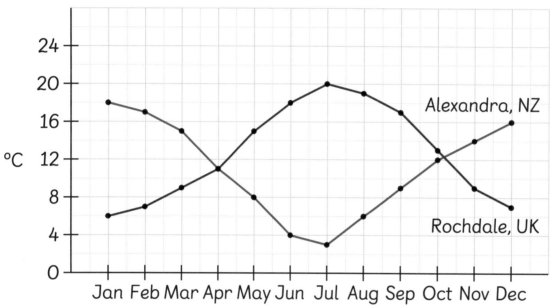

Average Monthly Temperature in Alexandra, NZ and Rochdale, UK (1980–2010)

What can we say about the temperatures in Alexandra and Rochdale?

Example

Alexandra is in the Southern Hemisphere and Rochdale is in the Northern Hemisphere.

This means that the hemispheres have opposite seasons. Summer in the Southern Hemisphere is winter in the Northern Hemisphere.

We can see that in spring and autumn, the temperatures are similar.

Month	Jan	Feb	Mar	Apr	May	Jun	Jul	Aug	Sep	Oct	Nov	Dec
Alexandra (°C)	18	17	15	11	8	4	3	6	9	12	14	16
Rochdale (°C)	6	7	9	11	15	18	20	19	17	13	9	7

The month with the greatest difference in temperatures was July.

In April, Alexandra and Rochdale had the same average monthly temperatures.

The lowest temperature in Alexandra was less than the lowest temperature in Rochdale.

The difference between Alexandra's lowest and highest temperatures was 15 °C.

1 Complete the table using the information shown on the graph.

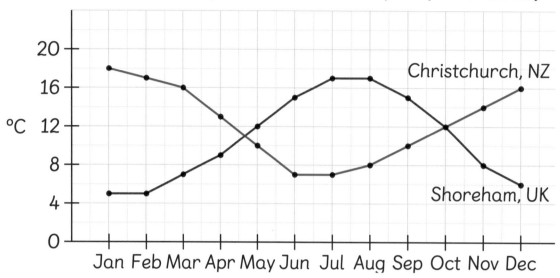

Average Monthly Temperature in
Christchurch, NZ and Shoreham, UK (1980–2010)

Month	Jan	Feb	Mar	Apr	May	Jun	Jul	Aug	Sep	Oct	Nov	Dec
Christchurch (°C)												
Shoreham (°C)												

2 Fill in the blanks using the information shown on the graph and in the table.

(a) The city with the highest average monthly temperature was

    [   ] .

(b) The difference between Christchurch and Shoreham's average

    temperatures in August was [   ] °C.

(c) The difference in Christchurch's highest and lowest temperatures

was [   ] °C.

(d) The difference in Shoreham's highest and lowest temperatures was

[   ] °C.

3 The line graph shows the cost of items in a bakery over a number of years.

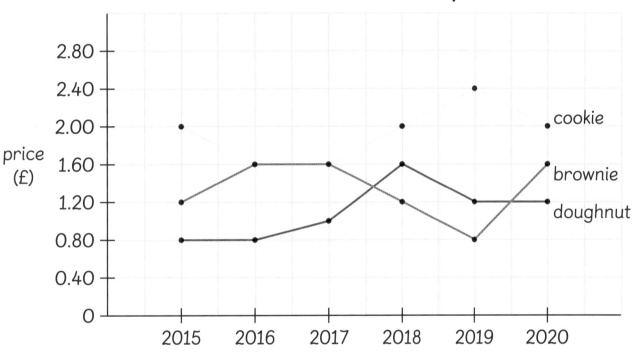

Price of Items in a Bakery

(a) The [   ] and [   ] were the same price in

2016 and 2017.

(b) The difference in price in 2019 between the brownie and the cookie

was £ [   ] .

(c) What was the difference in the price of a doughnut in 2015 and 2018?

£ [   ]

(d) In which year was the biggest difference between the price of a

brownie and the price of a doughnut? [   ]

Using millimetres and centimetres

Starter

Ruby is buying a new strap for her watch.

2 cm

18 mm

20 mm

22 mm

Which strap should Ruby buy?

Example

Ruby's watch needs a 2-cm wide strap.

The first strap is 18 mm wide.

2 cm = 20 mm

18 mm

10 mm = 1 cm
8 mm = 0.8 cm

The first strap is 1.8 cm.

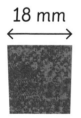

The first strap is 2 mm too small.

16

20 mm

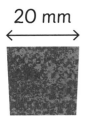

 20 mm = 2 cm

The second strap is 20 mm or 2 cm.
The second strap would fit Ruby's watch.

 20 ÷ 10 = 2

22 mm

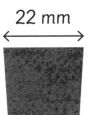

1 mm is 10 times smaller than 1 cm.

20 mm = 2 cm
2 mm = 0.2 cm
22 mm = 2.2 cm

2 ÷ 10 = 0.2

The third strap is
2 mm too wide.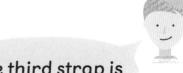

Practice

1 Convert centimetres to millimetres.

(a) 3 cm = ☐ mm

(b) 5 cm = ☐ mm

(c) 14 cm = ☐ mm

(d) 23 cm = ☐ mm

2 Convert millimetres to centimetres.

(a) 40 mm = ☐ cm

(b) 80 mm = ☐ cm

(c) 170 mm = ☐ cm

(d) 390 mm = ☐ cm

3 Convert the measurements.

(a) 16 mm = ☐ cm

(b) ☐ mm = 4.1 cm

(c) 13.8 cm = ☐ mm

(d) 102 mm = ☐ cm

Using centimetres and metres

Starter

I need to cut a piece of wood so it is 1.3 m long.

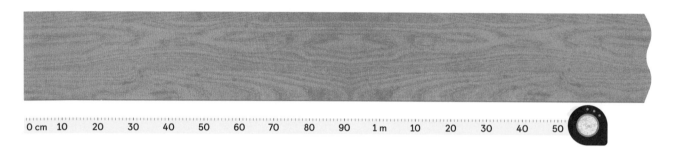

| 0 cm | 10 | 20 | 30 | 40 | 50 | 60 | 70 | 80 | 90 | 1 m | 10 | 20 | 30 | 40 | 50 |

Where should Emma cut the wood?

Example

100 cm = 1 m
30 cm = 0.3 m

$30 \div 100 = 0.3$

1 cm is 100 times smaller than 1 m.

130 cm = 1.3 m

1.3 m

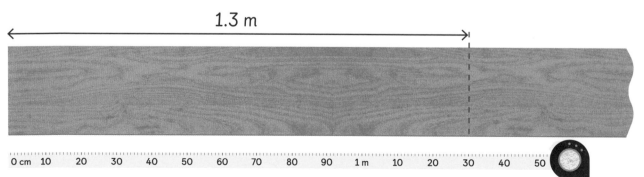

| 0 cm | 10 | 20 | 30 | 40 | 50 | 60 | 70 | 80 | 90 | 1 m | 10 | 20 | 30 | 40 | 50 |

What if the length of wood needed to be 2.13 m long?

$0.1 \times 100 = 10$

$0.03 \times 100 = 3$

2 m = 200 cm
0.1 m = 10 cm
0.03 m = 3 cm

2.13 m = 213 cm

1 m is 100 times greater than 1 cm.

Practice

1 Convert centimetres to metres.

(a) 300 cm = [　] m

(b) 250 cm = [　] m

(c) 458 cm = [　] m

(d) 909 cm = [　] m

2 Convert metres to centimetres.

(a) 46 m = [　] cm

(b) 3.4 m = [　] cm

(c) 18.5 m = [　] cm

(d) 20.9 m = [　] cm

3 Convert the measurements.

(a) 103 cm = [　] m

(b) 5.14 m = [　] cm

(c) 2004 cm = [　] m

(d) 48.09 m = [　] cm

Using metres and kilometres

Emma and her family are on holiday at a national park. They want to walk to the waterfall or the caves. Which walk is longer?

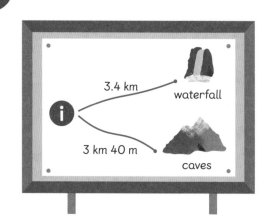

3.4 km — waterfall

3 km 40 m — caves

Example

Convert 3.4 km to metres.

0.1 km = 100 m
0.4 km = 400 m
3.4 km = 3000 m + 400 m
    = 3400 m

1 km = 1000 m
3 km = 3000 m

Convert 3 km 40 m to metres.

3 km 40 m = 3000 m + 40 m
    = 3040 m

The walk to the waterfall is longer.

There is another walk, which goes to the forest, that is 3010 m.
How many kilometres is that?

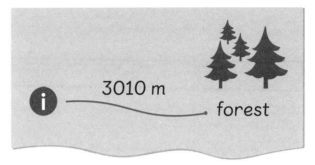

3010 = 3000 + 10
3000 m = 3 km
10 m = 0.01 km

1 km is 1000 times
greater than 1 m.

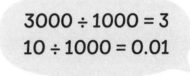

3000 ÷ 1000 = 3
10 ÷ 1000 = 0.01

3010 m = 3.01 km

Practice

1 Convert metres to kilometres.

(a) 6000 m = ☐ km

(b) 500 m = ☐ km

(c) 1200 m = ☐ km

(d) 20 m = ☐ km

2 Convert kilometres to metres.

(a) 7 km = ☐ m

(b) 6.4 km = ☐ m

(c) 5.03 km = ☐ m

(d) 1.001 km = ☐ m

3 Convert the distances.

(a) 3 km 50 m = ☐ m

(b) 1050 m = ☐ km ☐ m

(c) 11.3 km = ☐ m

(d) 45 km 5 m = ☐ km

Using grams and kilograms

Starter

Holly is using a recipe to make bread rolls.
Does she use more white flour or wholemeal flour?

Bread Rolls

0.4 kg	white flour
70 g	wholemeal flour
1 tsp	yeast
1 cup	water

Example

1 kg = 1000 g
0.1 kg = 100 g
0.4 kg = 400 g

1 kg is 1000 times greater that 1 g.

0.1 × 1000 = 100

Holly uses 0.4 kg or 400 g of white flour.

100 g = 0.1 kg
10 g = 0.01 kg
70 g = 0.07 kg

1 g is 1000 times smaller than 1 kg.

70 ÷ 1000 = 0.07

Holly uses 70 g or 0.07 kg of wholemeal flour.

She uses more white flour than wholemeal flour.

Practice

Complete the table.

Ingredient	Weight in kg and g	Weight in g	Weight in kg
rice	1 kg 300 g		
fish		2300 g	
onions	3 kg 50 g		
beans			2.98 kg
peppers	1 kg 60 g		
carrots		850 g	

Using seconds and minutes

Starter

> I put my popcorn in the microwave for 2 minutes 30 seconds.

> I put my popcorn in the microwave for 180 seconds.

Whose popcorn was in the microwave longer?

Example

> Convert 2 minutes 30 seconds to seconds.

1 min = 60 s
2 min = 120 s
2 min 30 s = 120 s + 30 s
          = 150 s
150 s < 180 s

's popcorn was in the microwave longer.

What is 180 seconds in minutes?

1 min = 60 s

3 × 6 = 18
3 × 60 = 180
3 min = 180 s

180 ÷ 60 = 3

3 min > 2 min 30 s

Practice

1 The time each kettle took to boil 2 cups of water is shown below. Show these times using minutes and seconds.

(a)

139 s

[ ] min [ ] s

(b)

129 s

[ ] min [ ] s

(c)

188 s

[ ] min [ ] s

2 Elliott chopped vegetables for 4 minutes 12 seconds before Ravi took over the chopping. Ravi then continued to chop the vegetables for 317 seconds.

(a) The total time Elliott and Ravi spent chopping vegetables was

[ ] minutes [ ] seconds.

(b) Ravi chopped vegetables for [ ] seconds longer than Elliott.

Using minutes and hours

Starter

A bread recipe has
the following instructions.
How many minutes
does it take in total to make
and bake the bread?

Bread Recipe

1. Mix the flour and water and
   leave for 20 minutes.
2. Add the yeast and salt and mix.
   Leave for 1 hour 40 minutes.
3. Knead the dough for 5 minutes
   then put it into baking tins.
   Leave the dough to rise in the
   tins for 1 hour 30 minutes.
4. Put the tins in the oven
   for 40 minutes.

Example

60 min = 1 h

There are 60
minutes in 1 hour.

Find the total amount of
time for the first 2 steps.

20 min + 1 h 40 min = 20 min + 60 min + 40 min
= 120 min

Find the total amount of
time for steps 3 and 4.

5 min + 1 h 30 min = 5 min + 60 min + 30 min
= 95 min

95 min + 40 min = 135 min

120 min + 135 min = 255 min

It takes 255 minutes in total to make
and bake the bread.

60 min = 1 h
120 min = 2 h
240 min = 4 h
255 min = 4 h 15 min

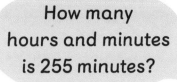

How many hours and minutes is 255 minutes?

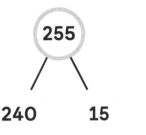

255

240   15

Practice

1 During the week Ravi writes down how
long he spends on his homework
for each subject.

English — 1 h 15 min
Maths — 1 h 15 min
Science — 35 min
History — 45 min

(a) How many minutes has Ravi spent
in total doing his homework?

1 h 15 min = [   ] min

[   ] + [   ] + [   ] + [   ] = [   ]

Ravi has spent [   ] minutes in total doing his homework.

(b) How many hours and minutes has Ravi spent in total doing
his homework?

[   ] min = [   ] h [   ] min

2 Convert the times.

(a) 240 min = [   ] h

(b) 3 h 10 min = [   ] min

(c) 105 min = [   ] h [   ] min

(d) 6 h 8 min = [   ] min

Using days and weeks

Oak is counting down the days until she goes on holiday.
Can you describe the number of days or weeks she has left until she goes?

March						2022
Sun	Mon	Tues	Wed	Thurs	Fri	Sat
		✕1	✕2	✕3	✕4	✕5
6	7	8	9	10	11	12
13	14	15	16	17	18	19
20	21	22	23	24	25	26
27	28	29	30	31		

Example

There are 7 days in 1 week.

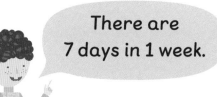

| 6 | 7 | 8 | 9 | 10 | 11 | 12 |

Oak has to wait 21 days until she goes on holiday.

$21 \div 7 = 3$

Oak has to wait 21 days or 3 weeks until she goes on holiday.

Hannah's grandmother has to wait 152 days until she sees Hannah.

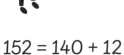

How many weeks does Hannah's grandmother have to wait?

152 = 140 + 12
140 ÷ 7 = 20
12 ÷ 7 = 1 remainder 5
152 ÷ 7 = 21 remainder 5

Look for the largest multiples of 7.

Hannah's grandmother has to wait 21 weeks 5 days until she sees Hannah.

Holly works out it is 225 days until she sees her cousins.
How many weeks and days is that?

Divide 225 by 7 to find the number of weeks.

The quotient, 32, is the number of weeks.

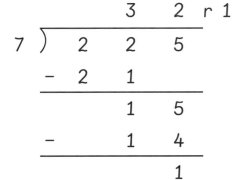

```
            3   2   r 1
7 )     2   2   5
    -   2   1
            1   5
    -       1   4
                1
```

The remainder, 1, is the number of days.

225 days is 32 weeks 1 day.

We can say it is approximately 32 weeks until Holly sees her cousins.

225 days ≈ 32 weeks

Practice

1 Charles starts camp on Monday 9 May. His last day at camp is Sunday 22 May. For how many weeks and days is Charles at camp?

May						2022
Sun	Mon	Tues	Wed	Thurs	Fri	Sat
1	2	3	4	5	6	7
8	9	10	11	12	13	14
15	16	17	18	19	20	21
22	23	24	25	26	27	28
29	30	31				

Charles is at camp for [ ] weeks [ ] days.

2 It takes a boat 59 days to sail from Southampton, UK, to Auckland, NZ.
How many weeks and days does it take to make the journey?

It takes the boat ☐ weeks ☐ days to make the journey.

3 It took a team of builders 165 days to build a house.
How many weeks and days did it take them to build the house?

$$\begin{array}{r} \square\,\square \ \ r\,\square \\ 7\,)\overline{\ 1\ \ 6\ \ 5\ } \end{array}$$

(a) The team of builders took ☐ weeks ☐ days to build
the house.

(b) The team of builders took approximately ☐ weeks to build
the house.

Using months and years

Starter

The number of months taken to build a space shuttle, submarine and cruise ship are shown below.

48 months

84 months

2 years 8 months

Which took the longest to build?

Example

There are 12 months in a year.

To convert months to years we can divide by 12.

48 months

12 months = 1 year
48 ÷ 12 = 4
48 months = 4 years
It took 4 years to build the space shuttle.

84 months

Divide 84 by 12.

$84 \div 12 = 7$
84 months = 7 years
It took 7 years to build the submarine.

Convert years and months to months.

2 years 8 months

1 year = 12 months

$2 \times 12 = 24$
2 years = 24 months
24 months + 8 months = 32 months
It took 32 months to build the cruise ship.

We can compare the lengths of time in years and months.

2 years 8 months, 4 years, 7 years

shortest ⟶ longest

We can also compare the lengths of time in months.

32 months, 48 months, 84 months

shortest ⟶ longest

The submarine took the longest time to build.

The building of the Petronas Twin Towers in Malaysia started in 1993.
It took 78 months from the day the building started to the day it opened.

How many years and months is 78 months?

```
              6  r 6
12 )     7    8
    –    7    2
             6
```

The quotient, 6, is the number of years.

The remainder, 6, is the number of months.

It took 6 years 6 months to build the Petronas Twin Towers.

1 Convert the lengths of time.

(a) 36 months = ☐ years

(b) 5 years = ☐ months

(c) 63 months = ☐ years ☐ months

(d) 2 years 4 months = ☐ months

2 Ruby's cousin is 67 months old.
Ravi's cousin is 2 years 5 months older than Ruby's cousin.
How old is Ravi's cousin?

Ravi's cousin is ☐ years ☐ months old.

3 Ravi's mum bought a car that was 14 months old. After 27 months of using the car she needed to change its tyres.
How old was the car when Ravi's mum changed its tyres?

The car was ☐ years ☐ months old.

Finding the volume of solids

Starter

Charles made these solids using 3 identical cubes for each one.

Do each of the solids take up the same amount of space?

Example

First, we need to find the space each cube fills.

Each cube has the same volume.

The 3 cubes take up the same amount of space, no matter how they are arranged.

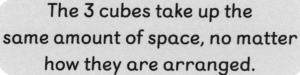

Each solid has a volume of 3 cubes.

We say that this is a cubic centimetre or 1 cm³.

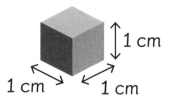

1 cm
1 cm
1 cm

Each edge is 1 cm.

Each of these solids has a volume of 4 cubic centimetres or 4 cm³.

The space that each of these solids fills is 4 cubic centimetres or 4 cm³.

Each solid has been made with 4 unit cubes.

Each unit cube is 1 cm³.

Each of the solids have been arranged differently but they all have the same volume.

The volume of each solid is 6 cubic centimetres or 6 cm³.

Practice

What is the volume of each solid?
Each cube is 1 cm³.

1

volume = [ ] cm³

2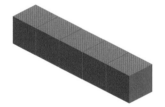

volume = [ ] cm³

3

volume = ⬜ cm³

4

volume = ⬜ cm³

5

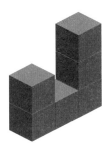

volume = ⬜ cm³

6

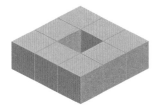

volume = ⬜ cm³

7

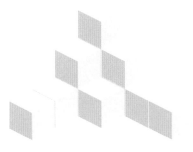

volume = ⬜ cm³

8

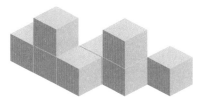

volume = ⬜ cm³

Finding capacity using cm³

Starter

 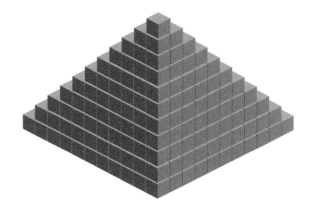

How can we use the cubes to find the capacity of the box?

Example

Each cube is 1 cm³.

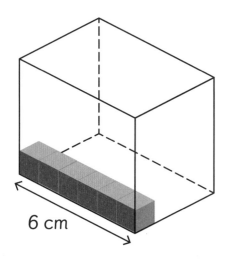

6 cm

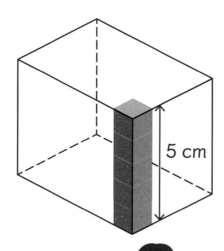

5 cm

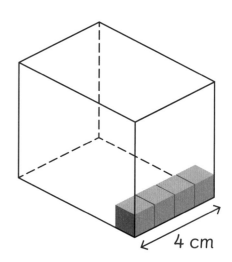

4 cm

We can find the number of cubes in a single layer by multiplying 6 by 4.

6 × 4 = 24

Each layer has 24 cubes.

There are 5 layers.

24 × 5 = 120
There are 120 cubes.

The capacity of the box is 120 cm³.

Practice

What is the capacity of each box?

1

2 cm

2 cm   2 cm

capacity = ___ cm³

2

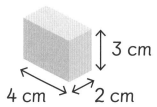

3 cm

4 cm   2 cm

capacity = ___ cm³

3

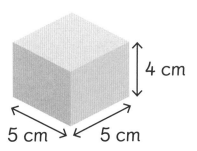

4 cm

5 cm   5 cm

capacity = ___ cm³

4

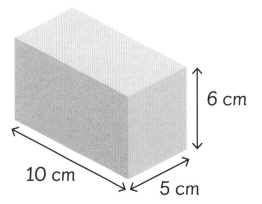

6 cm

10 cm   5 cm

capacity = ___ cm³

Review and challenge

1 The table shows the departure times of trains leaving Manchester Piccadilly station for Poynton.

Train Station	Departures				
Manchester Piccadilly	10:47	12:47	17:12	18:47	22:18
Stockport	10:57	12:57	17:25	18:57	22:29
Cheadle Hulme	11:01	13:01	17:32	19:01	22:33
Bramhall	11:04	13:04	17:35	19:04	22:37
Poynton	11:07	13:07	17:38	19:07	22:40

(a) How long is the 10:47 train journey from Manchester Piccadilly station to Cheadle Hulme? [ ] min

(b) Which trains can Hannah take from Stockport to arrive in Poynton after 6 p.m.? [ ] : [ ] and [ ] : [ ]

(c) The 17:12 train from Manchester Piccadilly station takes [ ] minutes longer to reach Bramhall than the 10:47 train from Manchester Piccadilly station to Bramhall.

2 Convert the measurements.

(a) 8 cm = [ ] mm

(b) [ ] cm = 40 mm

(c) 12 cm 3 mm = [ ] mm

(d) 73 mm = [ ] cm [ ] mm

(e) 3 m = [ ] cm

(f) [ ] m = 800 cm

(g) [ ] cm = 1 m 20 cm

(h) 904 cm = [ ] m [ ] cm

3 The line graph shows the number of items sold in a bakery at a train station and a bakery in a village in one day.

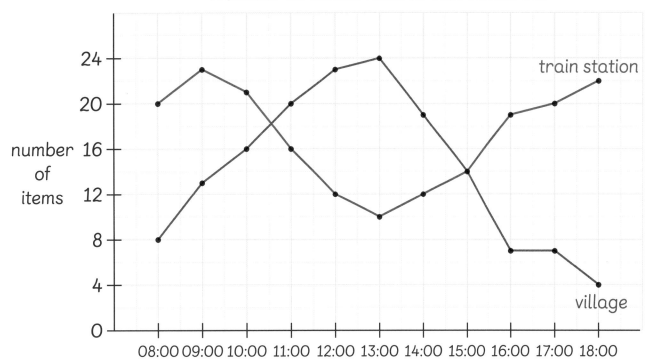

Number of Items Sold in Two Bakeries

(a) The greatest number of items sold at the village bakery was at _____ .

(b) The village bakery and the train station bakery sold the same number of items at _____ .

(c) The difference between the number of items sold at each bakery at 13:00 was _____ .

(d) The greatest difference between the number of items sold at each bakery happened at _____ .

4 Convert the distances.

(a) 7 km = _____ m

(b) 2000 m = _____ km

(c) 9 km 90 m = _____ m

(d) 3.5 km = _____ m

5 Convert the masses.

(a) 1000 g = [ ] kg

(b) 5 kg = [ ] g

(c) 3600 g = [ ] kg [ ] g

(d) 4 kg 5 g = [ ] g

6 Convert the times.

(a) 5 min = [ ] s

(b) 600 s = [ ] min

(c) 2 min 17 s = [ ] s

(d) 321 s = [ ] min [ ] s

(e) 2 h = [ ] min

(f) 360 min = [ ] h

(g) 4 h 23 min = [ ] min

(h) 96 min = [ ] h [ ] min

7 Convert the lengths of time.

(a) 19 days = [ ] weeks [ ] days

(b) 3 weeks 5 days = [ ] days

(c) 30 months = [ ] years [ ] months

(d) 5 years 10 months = [ ] months

8 What is the volume of each solid? Each cube is 1 cm³.

(a)

volume = [ ] cm³

(b)

volume = [ ] cm³

(c)

volume = [ ] cm³

(d)

volume = [ ] cm³

9 What is the capacity of each box?

(a)

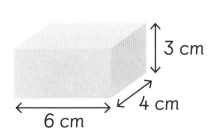

3 cm

4 cm

6 cm

capacity = [ ] cm³

(b)

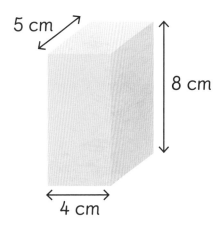

5 cm

8 cm

4 cm

capacity = [ ] cm³

10 Hannah's grandmother spent 1 year, 2 months (July and August), 6 weeks and 3 days in Australia before returning home.
For how many days was Hannah's grandmother in Australia?

Hannah's grandmother was in Australia for [ ] days.

Answers

Page 6   **1**

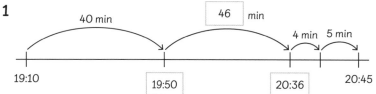

Sam's mum has 46 minutes to sit down and rest.

Page 7   **2**

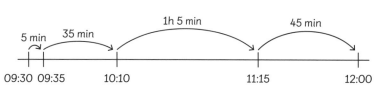

1 hour 5 minutes = 65 minutes
5 + 35 + 65 + 45 = 150
150 minutes = 2 hours 30 minutes
Mr Nightingale is at the gym for 2 hours 30 minutes.

3 15 + 40 + 55 = 110; 110 minutes = 1 hour 50 minutes. Amira's dad has spent 1 hour 50 minutes at the gym.

Page 10   **1 (a)** The month with the highest average temperature was January. **(b)** The months with the lowest average monthly temperature were June and July. **(c)** The difference between the highest and lowest average monthly temperatures was 11 °C. **(d)** The average monthly temperature decreased by 11 °C between January and June.

Page 11   **2 (a)** The difference in temperatures at 06:00 and 22:00 was 4 °C. **(b)** The temperature increased between 06:00 and 14:00. **(c)** The temperature decreased between 14:00 and 22:00. **(d)** Between 10:00 and 12:00, the temperature increased by 6 °C. **(e)** Between 16:00 and 22:00, the temperature decreased at a rate of 2 °C every 2 hours. **(f)** The temperature increased by 14 °C between 06:00 and 14:00.

Page 14   **1**

Month	Jan	Feb	Mar	Apr	May	Jun	Jul	Aug	Sep	Oct	Nov	Dec
Christchurch (°C)	18	17	16	13	10	7	7	8	10	12	14	16
Shoreham (°C)	5	5	7	9	12	15	17	17	15	12	8	6

2 (a) The city with the highest average monthly temperature was Christchurch. **(b)** The difference between Christchurch and Shoreham's average temperatures in August was 9 °C.

Page 15   **(c)** The difference in Christchurch's highest and lowest temperatures was 11 °C. **(d)** The difference in Shoreham's highest and lowest temperatures was 12 °C. **3 (a)** The brownie and cookie were the same price in 2016 and 2017. **(b)** The difference in price in 2019 between the brownie and the cookie was £1.60. **(c)** £0.80 **(d)** 2016

Page 17   **1 (a)** 3 cm = 30 mm **(b)** 5 cm = 50 mm **(c)** 14 cm = 140 mm **(d)** 23 cm = 230 mm
2 (a) 40 mm = 4 cm **(b)** 80 mm = 8 cm **(c)** 170 mm = 17 cm **(d)** 390 mm = 39 cm
3 (a) 16 mm = 1.6 cm **(b)** 41 mm = 4.1 cm **(c)** 13.8 cm = 138 mm **(d)** 102 mm = 10.2 cm

Page 19　**1 (a)** 300 cm = 3 m　**(b)** 250 cm = 2.5 m　**(c)** 458 cm = 4.58 m　**(d)** 909 cm = 9.09 m
2 (a) 46 m = 4600 cm　**(b)** 3.4 m = 340 cm　**(c)** 18.5 m = 1850 cm　**(d)** 20.9 m = 2090 cm
3 (a) 103 cm = 1.03 m　**(b)** 5.14 m = 514 cm　**(c)** 2004 cm = 20.04 m　**(d)** 48.09 m = 4809 cm

Page 21　**1 (a)** 6000 m = 6 km　**(b)** 500 m = 0.5 km　**(c)** 1200 m = 1.2 km　**(d)** 20 m = 0.02 km
2 (a) 7 km = 7000 m　**(b)** 6.4 km = 6400 m　**(c)** 5.03 km = 5030 m　**(d)** 1.001 km = 1001 m
3 (a) 3 km 50 m = 3050 m　**(b)** 1050 m = 1 km 50 m　**(c)** 11.3 km = 11 300 m
(d) 45 km 5 m = 45.005 km

Page 23

Ingredient	Weight in kg and g	Weight in g	Weight in kg
rice	1 kg 300 g	1300 g	1.3 kg
fish	2 kg 300 g	2300 g	2.3 kg
onions	3 kg 50 g	3050 g	3.05 kg
beans	2 kg 980 g	2980 g	2.98 kg
peppers	1 kg 60 g	1060 g	1.06 kg
carrots	0 kg 850 g	850 g	0.85 kg

Page 25　**1 (a)** 2 min 19 s　**(b)** 2 min 9 s　**(c)** 3 min 8 s　**2 (a)** The total time Elliott and Ravi spent chopping vegetables was 9 minutes 29 seconds.　**(b)** Ravi chopped vegetables for 65 seconds longer than Elliott.

Page 27　**1 (a)** 1 h 15 min = 75 min; 75 + 75 + 35 + 45 = 230; Ravi has spent 230 minutes in total doing his homework.　**(b)** 230 min = 3 h 50 min　**2 (a)** 240 min = 4 h　**(b)** 3 h 10 min = 190 min
(c) 105 min = 1 h 45 min　**(d)** 6 h 8 min = 368 min

Page 30　**1** Charles is at camp for 2 weeks 0 days.

Page 31　**2** It takes the boat 8 weeks 3 days to make the journey.

3
```
        2  3  r 4
  7 ) 1  6  5
    – 1  4
        2  5
    –   2  1
            4
```
(a) The team of builders took 23 weeks 4 days to build the house.
(b) The team of builders took approximately 24 weeks to build the house.

Page 35　**1 (a)** 36 months = 3 years　**(b)** 5 years = 60 months　**(c)** 63 months = 5 years 3 months
(d) 2 years 4 months = 28 months　**2** Ravi's cousin is 8 years 0 months old.　**3** The car was 3 years 5 months old.

Page 38　**1** 2 cm³　**2** 5 cm³

Page 39　**3** 7 cm³　**4** 6 cm³　**5** 6 cm³　**6** 8 cm³　**7** 12 cm³　**8** 8 cm³

Page 41　**1** 8 cm³　**2** 24 cm³　**3** 100 cm³　**4** 300 cm³

Answers continued

Page 42   **1 (a)** 14 min   **(b)** 18:57 and 22:29   **(c)** The 17:12 train from Manchester Piccadilly takes 6 minutes longer to reach Bramhall than the 10:47 train from Manchester Piccadilly to Bramhall.   **2 (a)** 8 cm = 80 mm   **(b)** 4 cm = 40 mm   **(c)** 12 cm 3 mm = 123 mm
(d) 73 mm = 7 cm 3 mm   **(e)** 3 m = 300 cm   **(f)** 8 m = 800 cm   **(g)** 120 cm = 1 m 20 cm
(h) 904 cm = 9 m 4 cm

Page 43   **3 (a)** The greatest number of items sold at the village bakery was at 13:00.
(b) The village bakery and the train station bakery sold the same number of items at 15:00.
(c) The difference between the number of items sold at each bakery at 13:00 was 14.
(d) The greatest difference between the number of items sold at each bakery happened at 18:00.   **4 (a)** 7 km = 7000 m   **(b)** 2000 m = 2 km   **(c)** 9 km 90 m = 9090 m   **(d)** 3.5 km = 3500 m

Page 44   **5 (a)** 1000 g = 1 kg   **(b)** 5 kg = 5000 g   **(c)** 3600 g = 3 kg 600 g   **(d)** 4 kg 5 g = 4005 g
6 (a) 5 min = 300 s   **(b)** 600 s = 10 min   **(c)** 2 min 17 s = 137 s   **(d)** 321 s = 5 min 21 s
(e) 2 h = 120 min   **(f)** 360 min = 6 h   **(g)** 4 h 23 min = 263 min   **(h)** 96 min = 1 h 36 min
7 (a) 19 days = 2 weeks 5 days   **(b)** 3 weeks 5 days = 26 days   **(c)** 30 months = 2 years 6 months
(d) 5 years 10 months = 70 months   **8 (a)** 4 cm³   **(b)** 5 cm³

Page 45   **(c)** 7 cm³   **(d)** 5 cm³   **9 (a)** 72 cm³   **(b)** 160 cm³   **10** Hannah's grandmother was in Australia for 472 days.